Eyelet Rows Shawl

Easy

MEASUREMENTS
Width along upper edge 68"/172.5cm
Length at center 30"/76cm

MATERIALS
Yarn
Any sock-weight wool, approx 1¾oz/50g, 170yd/155m per skein
• 4 skeins in Variegated Earth Tones

Needle
• One size 7 (4.5mm) circular needle, 40"/100cm long, *or size to obtain gauge*

Notions
• Stitch marker

GAUGE
17 sts and 36 rows to 4"/10cm over garter st using size 7 (4.5mm) needles.
TAKE TIME TO CHECK YOUR GAUGE.

NOTES
1) Slip all sts purlwise.
2) Circular needle is used to accommodate large number of sts. Do *not* join.

SHAWL
Cast on 5 sts using the cable cast-on.
Set-up row 1 (RS) [Kfb] twice, pm, kfb, k1, sl 1 wyib—8 sts.
Set-up row 2 Pfb, k2, p1, sm, k3, sl 1 wyif—9 sts.

Begin Garter Section
Garter row 1 Kfb, k to 1 st before marker, kfb, sm, kfb, k to last st, sl 1 wyib—3 sts inc'd.
Garter row 2 Pfb, k to 1 st before marker, p1, sm, k to last st, sl 1 wyif—1 st inc'd.
Rep garter rows 1 and 2 six times more—37 sts.

Begin Lace Rib
Row 1 (RS) Kfb, *k2, p2; rep from * to 1 st before marker, kfb, sm, kfb, k1, *p2, k2; rep from * to last st, sl 1 wyib—3 sts inc'd.
Row 2 Pfb, *p2, k2; rep from * to 3 sts before marker, p3, sm, *p2, k2; rep from * to last 4 sts, p2, k1, sl 1 wyif—1 st inc'd.
Row 3 Kfb, p1, *k2, p2; rep from * to 2 sts before marker, k1, kfb, sm, kfb, *k2, p2; rep from * to last 4 sts, k2, p1, sl 1 wyib—3 sts inc'd.
Row 4 Pfb, k1, *p2, k2; rep from * to 4 sts before marker, p2, k1, p1, sm, k1, *p2, k2; rep from * to last st, sl 1 wyif—1 st inc'd.
Row 5 Kfb, *p2, k2tog, yo; rep from * to 1 st before marker, pfb, sm, kfb, p1, *yo, ssk, p2; rep from * to last st, sl 1 wyib—3 sts inc'd.
Row 6 Pfb, *k2, p2; rep from * to 3 sts before marker, k2, p1, sm, *k2, p2; rep from * to last 4 sts, k2, p1, sl 1 wyif—1 st inc'd.
Row 7 Kfb, k1, *p2, yo, ssk; rep from * to 2 sts before marker, p1, pfb, sm, kfb, *p2, k2tog, yo; rep from * to last 4 sts, p2, k1, sl 1 wyib—3 sts inc'd.
Row 8 Pfb, p1, *k2, p2; rep from * to marker, sm, p1, *k2, p2; rep from * to last st, sl 1 wyif—1 st inc'd.
Rows 9–12 Rep rows 1–4—61 sts.
[Work garter rows 1 and 2 eight times, then work rows 1–12 of lace rib] 4 times more, then work garter rows 1 and 2 eight times, then work rows 1–11 of lace rib once more—340 sts.
Bind off in pat.

FINISHING
Weave in ends. Block to measurements.•

Contents

Malibu Ripple Shawl 2

Eyelet Rows Shawl 4

Going Your Way Shawl 6

Shell Lace Shawl 9

Diamond Lace Shawl 10

Textured Trails Shawl 12

Mesh Shawl 15

Diagonal Ridge Shawl 16

Swiss Shawl 18

Garter Spine Shawl 21

Arrow Shawl 22

Texture Trio Shawl 24

Four-Triangle Shawl 26

Sideways Ridge Shawl 28

Horizontal Stripes Shawl 30

Color Swap Shawl 32

Open Waves Shawl 35

Duality Shawl 36

Garter and Lace Shawl 38

Rainbow Shawl 40

Malibu Ripple Shawl

Easy

MEASUREMENTS
Width along upper edge 54"/137cm
Length at center 28"/71cm

MATERIALS
Yarn
Any DK-weight cotton, approx 3½oz/100g, 220yd/200m per skein (3)
• 3 skeins in Variegated Turquoise (A)
• 1 skein in White (B)

Needles
• One size 6 (4mm) circular needle, 32"/80cm long, *or size to obtain gauge*

Notions
• Stitch marker

GAUGE
21 sts and 28 rows to 4"/10cm over St st using size 6 (4mm) needle.
TAKE TIME TO CHECK YOUR GAUGE.

NOTE
Circular needle is used to accommodate large number of sts. Do *not* join.

SHAWL
With A, cast on 7 sts.
Row 1 (RS) K3, yo, k1, yo, k3—9 sts.
Row 2 K3, p to last 3 sts, p3.
Row 3 K3, yo, k1, yo, pm, [k1, yo] twice, k3—13 sts.
Row 4 Rep row 2.
Row 5 K3, yo, k to marker, yo, sm, k1, yo, k to last 3 sts, yo, k3—4 sts inc'd.
Row 6 Rep row 2.
Rep rows 5 and 6 twelve times more, then rep row 5 once more—69 sts.
Next inc row (WS) K3, p1, [M1 p-st, p5] 12 times, p2, k3—81 sts.

Begin Wave Pattern
Row 1 (RS) K3, yo, *[k2tog] 3 times, [k1, yo] 6 times, [k2tog] 3 times; rep from * to 1 st before marker, k1, yo, sm, k1, yo, k1, **[k2tog] 3 times, [yo, k1] 6 times, [k2tog] 3 times; rep from ** to last 3 sts, yo, k3—85 sts.
Rows 2, 4, 6, 8, & 10 K3, p to last 3 sts, k3.
Row 3 K3, yo, k to 1 st before marker, yo, sm, k1, yo, k to last 3 sts, yo, k3—89 sts.
Row 5 K3, yo, k2, *[k2tog] 3 times, [k1, yo] 6 times, [k2tog] 3 times; rep from * to 3 sts before marker, k3, yo, sm, k1, yo, k3, **[k2tog] 3 times, [yo, k1] 6 times, [k2tog] 3 times; rep from ** to last 5 sts, k2, yo, k3—93 sts.
Row 7 Rep row 3—97 sts.
Row 9 K3, yo, k4, *[k2tog] 3 times, [k1, yo] 6 times, [k2tog] 3 times; rep from * to 5 sts before marker, k5, yo, sm, k1, yo, k5, **[k2tog] 3 times, [yo, k1] 6 times, [k2tog] 3 times; rep from ** to last 7 sts, k4, yo, k3—101 sts.
Row 11 Rep row 3—105 sts.
Row 12 Knit.
Rows 13–16 With B, rep rows 11 and 12 twice—113 sts.
Row 17 With A, rep row 11—117 sts.
Row 18 Rep row 2.
Row 19 K3, yo, [k1, yo] 3 times, [k2tog] 6 times, *[k1, yo] 6 times, [k2tog] 6 times; rep from * to 4 sts before marker, [k1, yo] 4 times, sm, k1, [yo, k1] 4 times, [k2tog] 6 times, **[yo, k1] 6 times, [k2tog] 6 times; rep from ** to last 6 sts, [yo, k1] 4 times, k2—121 sts.
Rows 20, 22, 24, 26, & 28 Rep row 2.
Row 21 Rep row 3—125 sts.
Row 23 K3, yo, k3, [yo, k1] twice, yo, [k2tog] 6 times, *[k1, yo] 6 times, [k2tog] 6 times; rep from * to 6 sts before marker, [k1, yo] 3 times, k3, yo, sm, k1, yo, k3, [yo, k1] 3 times, [k2tog] 6 times, **[yo, k1] 6 times, [k2tog] 6 times; rep from ** to last 8 sts, [yo, k1] 3 times, k2, yo, k3—129 sts.
Row 25 Rep row 3—133 sts.
Row 27 K3, yo, k5, [yo, k1] twice, yo, [k2tog] 6 times, *[k1, yo] 6 times, [k2tog] 6 times; rep from * to 8 sts before marker, [k1, yo] 3 times, k5, yo, sm, k1, yo, k5, [yo, k1] 3 times, [k2tog] 6 times, **[yo, k1] 6 times, [k2tog] 6 times; rep from ** to last 10 sts, [yo, k1] 3 times, k4, yo, k3—137 sts.
Rows 29–36 Rep rows 11 to 18—153 sts.
Rep rows 1–36 for wave pat twice more, then work rows 1–34 once more—365 sts. With B, cast off evenly knitwise.

FINISHING
Weave in ends. Block to measurements.•

Going Your Way Shawl

Intermediate

MEASUREMENTS
Width along upper edge 84"/213.5cm
Length at center 30"/76 cm

MATERIALS
Yarn
Any worsted-weight acrylic/nylon/mohair/wool blend with sequins and beads, approx 3½oz/100g, 188yd/169m per skein
• 4 skeins in Purple

Needles
• One size 7 (4.5mm) circular needle, 40"/100cm long, *or size to obtain gauges*

Notions
• Removable stitch marker

GAUGES
• 20 sts and 30 rows to 4"/10cm over St st using size 7 (4.5mm) needles.
• 15 sts and 30 rows to 4"/10cm over lace pats using size 7 (4.5mm) needles.
TAKE TIME TO CHECK YOUR GAUGES.

STITCH GLOSSARY
M1R Insert LH needle from back to front under the strand between last st worked and next st on LH needle. K into the front loop to twist the st.
M1L Insert LH needle from front to back under the strand between last st worked and next st on LH needle. K into the back loop to twist the st.

OUTWARD LACE PATTERN
(over a multiple of 3 sts plus 4)
Row 1 (RS) K3, M1R, ssk, yo, *k1, ssk, yo; rep from * to 2 sts before marked st, k2, M1R, k1 (center st), M1L, k2, **yo, k2tog, k1; rep from ** to last 5 sts, yo, k2tog, M1L, k3—4 sts inc'd.
Row 2 and all WS rows K3, p to last 3 sts, k3.
Row 3 K3, M1R, *ssk, yo, k1; rep from * to marked st, M1R, k1 (center st), M1L, **k1, yo, k2tog; rep from ** to last 3 sts, M1L, k3—4 sts inc'd.
Row 5 K3, M1R, ssk, *yo, k1, ssk; rep from * to marked st, yo, M1R, k1 (center st), M1L, yo, **k2tog, k1, yo; rep from ** to last 5 sts, k2tog, M1L, k3—4 sts inc'd.
Row 6 Rep row 2.
Rep rows 1–6 for outward lace pat.

INWARD LACE PATTERN
(over a multiple of 3 sts plus 4)
Row 1 (RS) K3, M1R, k2, *yo, k2tog, k1; rep from * to last 2 sts before marked st, yo, k2tog, M1R, k1 (center st), M1L, ssk, yo, **k1, ssk, yo; rep from ** to last 5 sts, k2, M1L, k3—4 sts inc'd.
Row 2 and all WS rows K3, p to last 3 sts, k3.
Row 3 K3, M1R, *k1, yo, k2tog; rep from * to marked st, M1R, k1 (center st), M1L, **ssk, yo, k1; rep from ** to last 3 sts, M1L, k3—4 sts inc'd.
Row 5 K3, M1R, yo, *k2tog, k1, yo; rep from * to last 2 sts before marked st, k2tog, M1R, k1 (center st), M1L, ssk, **yo, k1, ssk; rep from ** to last 3 sts, yo, M1L, k3—4 sts inc'd.
Row 6 Rep row 2.
Rep rows 1–6 for inward lace pat.

NOTE
Move stitch marker up on center st as work progresses.

SHAWL
Cast on 3 sts. Knit 6 rows.
With RS facing, turn work 90 degrees clockwise and pick up and k 3 sts from side of piece (1 st in each garter ridge), then pick up and k 3 sts from cast-on edge—9 sts.

Stockinette Band 1
Set-up row (WS) K3 (selvage sts), k2, pm on last st worked (center st), k1, k3 (selvage sts).
St st pat row 1 (RS) K3, M1R, k to marked st, M1R, k1 (marked center st), M1L, k to last 3 sts, M1L, k3—4 sts inc'd.
St st pat row 2 K3, p to last 3 sts, k3.
Rep st st pat rows 1 and 2 fourteen times more, then rep row 1 once more—73 sts.
Dec row (WS) K3, p to last 3 sts, dec'ing 16 sts evenly across to last 3 sts, k3—57 sts.

Lace Band 1
Rep rows 1–6 of outward lace pat twice—81 sts.
Rep rows 1–6 of inward lace pat twice—105 sts.

Stockinette Band 2
Inc row (RS) K3, M1R, [k4, M1] 12 times, k1, M1R, k1 (marked center st), M1L, k1, [M1, k4] 12 times, M1L, k3—28 sts inc'd and 133 sts in total.
Next row Rep St st pat row 2.
Rep St st pat rows 1 and 2 six times, then row 1 once more—161 sts.
Dec row (WS) K3, p to last 3 sts, dec'ing 38 sts evenly across to last 3 sts, k3—123 sts.

Lace Band 2
Rep rows 1–6 of outward lace pat 3 times—159 sts.
Rep rows 1–6 of inward lace pat 3 times—195 sts.

Going Your Way Shawl

Stockinette Band 3
Inc row (RS) K3, M1R, k2, [M1, k4] 22 times, [M1, k2] twice, M1R, k1 (marked center st), M1L, [k2, M1] twice, [k4, M1] 22 times, k2, M1L, k3—52 sts inc'd and 247 sts in total.
Next row Rep St st pat row 2.
Rep St st pat rows 1 and 2 six times, then row 1 once more—275 sts.
Dec row (WS) K3, p to last 3 sts, dec'ing 68 sts evenly across to last 3 sts, k3—207 sts.

Lace Band 3
Rep rows 1–6 of outward lace pat twice—231 sts.
Rep rows 1–6 of inward lace pat twice—255 sts.

Stockinette Band 4
Inc row (RS) K3, M1R, [k3, M1] 41 times, k1, M1R, k1 (marked center st), M1L, k1, [M1, k3] 41 times, M1L, k3—86 sts inc'd and 341 sts in total.
Next row Rep St st pat row 2.
Rep St st pat rows 1 and 2 six times—365 sts.

Border
Row 1 (RS) K to center st, M1R, k1 (center st), M1L, k to end—2 sts inc'd.
Row 2 Knit.
Rep rows 1 and 2 twice more—371 sts. Bind off.

FINISHING
Weave in ends. Block to measurements.•

Shell Lace Shawl

Easy

MEASUREMENTS
Width 17"/43cm
Length 66"/168cm

MATERIALS
Yarn
Any worsted-weight alpaca/wool blend, approx 3½oz/100g, 164yd/150m per skein
• 5 skeins in White

Needles
• One pair size 6 (4mm) needles, *or size to obtain gauge*

GAUGE
18 sts and 27 rows to 4"/10cm over lace pat using size 6 (4mm) needles.
TAKE TIME TO CHECK YOUR GAUGE.

SHAWL
Cast on 78 sts. Knit 6 rows.

Begin Lace Pattern
Row 1 (RS) Knit.
Row 2 K3 (garter border), p to last 3 sts, k3 (garter border).
Row 3 K5, *yo, p1, p3tog, p1, yo, k2; rep from * to last 3 sts, k3.
Row 4 Rep row 2.
Rep rows 1–4 for lace pat (with 3 sts each side in garter st) until piece measures approx 65"/165cm from beg, end with a row 4.
Knit 6 rows. Bind off.

FINISHING
Weave in ends. Block to measurements.•

Diamond Lace Shawl

Intermediate

MEASUREMENTS
Width (around outside edge, after blocking) 45"/114.5cm
Depth (at deepest point, after blocking) 15"/38cm

MATERIALS
Yarn
Any DK-weight wool, approx 2oz/57g hanks, 200yd/183m per skein ③
• 2 skeins in Aqua

Needles
• One size 7 (4.5mm) circular needle, 29"/74cm long, *or size to obtain gauge*

GAUGE
18 sts and 26 rows to 4"/10cm over St st, after blocking, using size 7 (4.5mm) needle.
TAKE TIME TO CHECK YOUR GAUGE.

SHORT ROW WRAP & TURN (w&t)
on RS row (on WS row)
1) Wyib (wyif), sl next st purlwise.
2) Move yarn between the needles to the front (back).
3) Sl the same st back to LH needle. Turn work. One st is wrapped.
4) When working the wrapped st, insert RH needle under the wrap and work it tog with the corresponding st on needle.

NOTE
Circular needle is used to accommodate large number of sts. Do *not* join.

SHAWL
Cast on 284 sts. Purl 1 row on WS.

Row 1 (RS) K2, work row 1 of chart 1, working 10-st rep 28 times, k2.
Row 2 K2, work row 2 of chart 1, working 10-st rep 28 times, k2.
Cont in pats as established, keeping first and last 2 sts in garter st (k every row) until 18 rows of chart have been worked.

Begin Chart 2
Row 1 (RS) K2, work row 1 of chart 2, working 2-st rep to last 2 sts, k2.
Row 2 K2, work row 2 of chart 2 to last 2 sts, k2.
Cont in pats as established, keeping first and last 2 sts in garter st (k every row) until 4 rows of chart have been worked.

Short Row Shaping
Set-up row 1 (RS) K152, w&t.
Set-up row 2 P20, w&t.
Row 1 (RS) K to 1 st before previous wrap, k2tog, k3, w&t.
Row 2 (WS) P to 1 st before previous wrap, p2tog, p3, w&t.
Rep last 2 rows 33 times more and all sts have been worked. Bind off firmly knitwise on RS.

FINISHING
Weave in ends. Block to measurements, pinning out points of diamonds on cast-on edge to form a scalloped edge.•

CHART 1

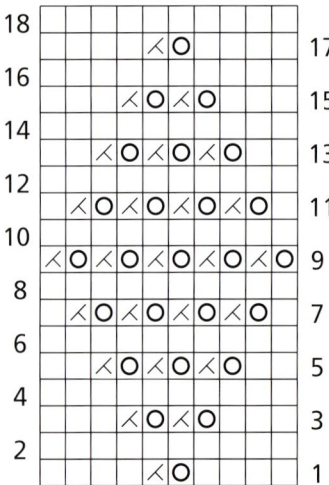

10-st rep

CHART 2

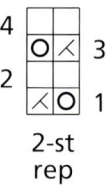

2-st rep

STITCH KEY
☐ k on RS, p on WS
⊠ k2tog
○ yo

Textured Trails Shawl

Intermediate

MEASUREMENTS
Width 60"/152.5cm
Depth at center 17"/43cm

MATERIALS
Yarn
Any DK-weight superwash wool, approx 3½oz/100g, 263yd/240m per skein
• 2 skeins in Variegated Green

NEEDLES
• One size 6 (4mm) circular needle, 40"/100cm long, *or size to obtain gauge*

NOTIONS
• Stitch markers

GAUGE
20 sts and 22 rows to 4"/10cm over trails pat using size 6 (4mm) needle.
TAKE TIME TO CHECK YOUR GAUGE.

STITCH GLOSSARY
kyok (Knit 1 through front loop, yo, knit 1 through back loop) into next st—2 sts inc'd.

TRAILS PATTERN
(over 25 sts)
Row 1 K1, yo, k4, k2tog, k11, ssk, k4, yo, k1.
Row 2 P2, k4, p13, k4, p2.
Row 3 K2, yo, k4, k2tog, k9, ssk, k4, yo, k2.
Row 4 P3, k4, p11, k4, p3.
Row 5 K3, yo, k4, k2tog, k7, ssk, k4, yo, k3.
Row 6 P4, k4, p9, k4, p4.
Row 7 K4, yo, k4, k2tog, k5, ssk, k4, yo, k4.
Row 8 P5, k4, p7, k4, p5.
Row 9 K5, yo, k4, k2tog, k3, ssk, k4, yo, k5.
Row 10 P6, k4, p5, k4, p6.
Row 11 K6, yo, k4, k2tog, k1, ssk, k4, yo, k6.
Row 12 P7, k4, p3, k4, p7.
Row 13 K7, yo, k4, S2KP, k4, yo, k7.
Row 14 P8, k4, p1, k4, p8.
Rows 15–17 Knit.
Row 18 Purl.
Row 19 Knit.
Row 20 Purl.
Rows 21 and 22 Knit.
Rep rows 1–22 for trails pat.

NOTES
1) Trails pattern may be worked from text or chart (see page 14).
2) Increases are worked inside 2-st garter borders each side as yo's on RS, and as kyok's on WS rows. Kyok's are worked into yo from previous row.
3) Place a stitch marker on RS of work to help keep track of rows.
4) Circular needle is used to accommodate large number of sts. Do *not* join.

SHAWL
Cast on 5 sts.
Row 1 K2, yo, k to last 2 sts, yo, k2—2 sts inc'd.
Row 2 K2, kyok, k to last 3 sts, kyok, k2—4 sts inc'd.
Rep rows 1 and 2 four times more—35 sts.

Begin Trails Pattern
Tier 1
Row 1 (RS) K2, yo, k3, pm, work trails pat over 25 sts, pm, k3, yo, k2—37 sts.
Row 2 K2, kyok, k to marker, sm, work trails pat to marker, sm, k to last 3 sts, kyok, k2—41 sts.
Row 3 K2, yo, k to marker, sm, work trails pat to marker, sm, k to last 2 sts, yo, k2—2 sts inc'd.
Row 4 K2, kyok, k to marker, sm, work trails pat to marker, sm, k to last 3 sts, kyok, k2—4 sts inc'd.
Cont to work pattern in this way, working yo inc's on RS rows and kyok inc's on WS rows, through row 20 of trails pat—95 sts.
Row 21 (RS) K2, yo, k to last 2 sts, yo, k2—97 sts.
Row 22 K2, kyok, k8, pm, k25, sm, k25, sm, k25, pm, k8, kyok, k2—101 sts.

Textured Trails Shawl

Tier 2
Row 1 (RS) K2, yo, k to marker, [sm, work trails pat over 25 sts] 3 times, sm, k to last 2 sts, yo, k2—2 sts inc'd.
Row 2 K2, kyok, k to marker, [sm, work trails pat over 25 sts] 3 times, sm, k to last 3 sts, kyok, k2—4 sts inc'd.
Cont in pats as established through row 20 of trails pat—161 sts.
Row 21 (RS) K2, yo, k to last 2 sts, yo, k2—163 sts.
Row 22 K2, kyok, k16, pm, k25, [sm, k25] 4 times, pm, k16, kyok, k2—167 sts.

Tier 3
Row 1 (RS) K2, yo, k to marker, [sm, work trails pat over 25 sts] 5 times, sm, k to last 2 sts, yo, k2—2 sts inc'd.
Row 2 K2, kyok, k to marker, [sm, work trails pat over 25 sts] 5 times, sm, k to last 3 sts, kyok, k2—4 sts inc'd.
Cont in pats as established through row 20 of trails pat—227 sts.
Row 21 (RS) K2, yo, k to last 2 sts, yo, k2—229 sts.
Row 22 K2, kyok, k24, pm, k25, [sm, k25] 5 times, sm, k25, pm, k24, kyok, k2—233 sts.

Tier 4
Row 1 (RS) K2, yo, k2, pm, [work trails pat over 25 sts, sm] 9 times, pm after last rep, k2, yo, k2—2 sts inc'd.
Row 2 K2, kyok, k to marker, [sm, work trails pat over 25 sts] 9 times, sm, k to last 3 sts, kyok, k2—4 sts inc'd.
Cont in pats as established through row 20 of trails pat—293 sts.
Row 21 (RS) K2, yo, k to last 2 sts, yo, k2—295 sts.
Row 22 K2, kyok, k7, pm, k25, [sm, k25] 9 times, sm, k25, pm, k7, kyok, k2—299 sts.

Tier 5
Row 1 (RS) K2, yo, k to marker, [sm, work trails pat over 25 sts] 11 times, sm, k to last 2 sts, yo, k2—2 sts inc'd.
Row 2 K2, kyok, k to marker, [sm, work trails pat over 25 sts] 11 times, sm, k to last 3 sts, kyok, k2—4 sts inc'd.
Cont in pats as established through row 16 of trails pat—347 sts.

I-cord Bind-Off
Cast on 3 sts. *K2, k2tog, working rem cast-on st tog with next st from shawl edge, slip 3 sts back to LH needle; rep from * until all sts are bound off.

FINISHING
Weave in ends. Block lightly to measurements, keeping curves along bound-off edge.•

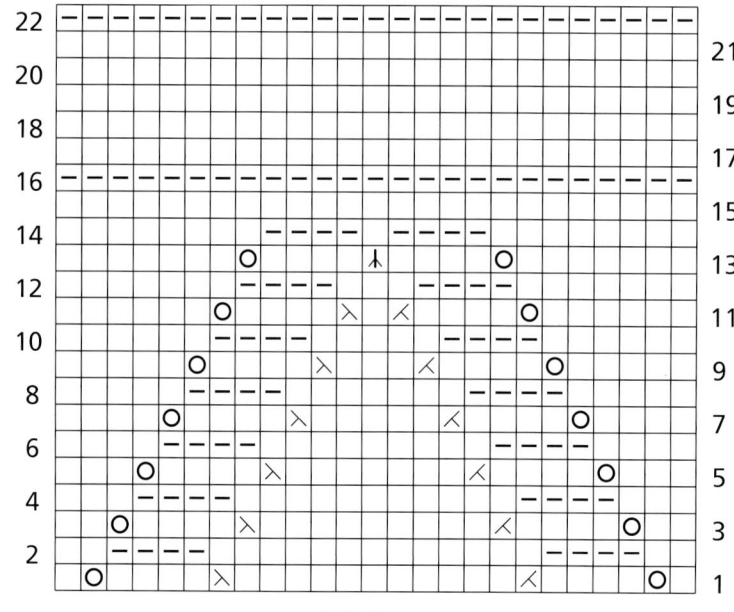

STITCH KEY
- □ k on RS, p on WS
- — p on RS, k on WS
- O yo
- ⧄ k2tog
- ⧅ ssk
- ⋏ S2KP

25-st rep

Mesh Shawl

Easy

MEASUREMENTS
Width 67"/170cm
Length 12½"/31.5cm

MATERIALS
Yarn
Any worsted-weight cotton/acrylic blend, approx 5.3oz/150g, 518yd/473m per skein (4)
• 1 skein in Blue/White Gradient

Needles
• One size 8 (5mm) circular needle, 40"/100cm long, *or size to obtain gauge*

GAUGE
12 sts and 26 rows to 4"/10cm in right or left slanting eyelet pat using size 8 (5mm) needles.
TAKE TIME TO CHECK YOUR GAUGE.

LEFT SLANTING EYELET
(over an even number of sts)
Row 1 (RS) K1, *k2tog, yo; rep from * to last st, k1.
Row 2 Purl.
Rep rows 1 and 2 for left slanting eyelet pat.

RIGHT SLANTING EYELET
(over an even number of sts)
Row 1 (RS) K1, *yo, ssk; rep from * to last st, k1.
Row 2 Purl.
Rep rows 1 and 2 for right slanting eyelet pat.

NOTES
1) Shawl is knit widthwise.
2) Circular needle is used to accommodate large number of sts. Do *not* join.

SHAWL
Cast on 204 sts.
Work in rev St st (p on RS, k on WS) for 8 rows, end with a WS row.

Eyelet Band 1
Work left slanting eyelet pat for 6 rows.
Work right slanting eyelet pat for 4 rows.
Work 4 rows in rev St st.

Eyelet Band 3
Work left slanting eyelet pat for 16 rows.
Work right slanting eyelet pat for 14 rows.
Work 4 rows in rev St st.

Eyelet Band 3
Work left slanting eyelet pat for 14 rows.
Work right slanting eyelet pat for 12 rows.
Work 8 rows in rev St st.
Bind off.

FINISHING
Weave in ends. Block gently to measurements.•

Diagonal Ridge Shawl

Intermediate

MEASUREMENTS
Width along upper edge 50"/127cm
Length 34"/86.5cm

MATERIALS
Yarn
Any bulky-weight superwash wool, approx 3½oz/100g, 127yd/116m per skein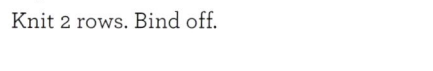
• 5 skeins in Yellow

Needle
• One size 10 (6mm) circular needle, 40"/100cm long, or size to obtain gauge

GAUGE
14 sts and 24 rows to 4"/10cm over chevron and ridge pats using size 10 (6mm) needles.
TAKE TIME TO CHECK YOUR GAUGE.

NOTES
1) Shawl uses all 5 skeins. It may be necessary to unravel gauge swatch.
2) Circular needle is used to accommodate large number of sts. Do *not* join.

SHAWL
Center Panel
Cast on 45 sts. Knit 1 row.

Begin chevron pattern
Rows 1 and 3 (RS) Kfb, k20, S2KP, k20, kfb.
Row 2 K1, p to last st, k1.
Ridge row 4 Rep row 1.
Rep rows 1–4 for chevron pat 29 times more. Piece measures approx 34"/86.5cm.

Fill top of chevron
Row 1 Knit.
Row 2 K1, p to last st, k1.
Row 3 K24, k2tog, k1, turn.
Row 4 Sl 1, p4, p2tog, p1, turn.
Row 5 Sl 1, k5, k2tog, k1, turn.
Row 6 Sl 1, p6, p2tog, p1, turn.
Row 7 Sl 1, k to 1 st before previous turn, k2tog, k1, turn.
Row 8 Sl 1, k to 1 st before previous turn, p2tog, p1, turn.

Rep rows 7 and 8 seven times more—25 sts. Knit 2 rows. Bind off.

Left Side Triangle
With RS facing, beg at bound off edge, pick up and k 95 sts along left side of center panel to cast-on edge. Knit 1 row on WS.

Begin ridge pattern
Rows 1 and 3 (RS) K to last 3 sts, ssk, k1.
Row 2 K1, ssp, p to last st, k1.
Ridge row 4 Knit.
Rep rows 1–4 until 2 sts rem. Bind off.

Right Side Triangle
With RS facing, beg at cast-on edge, pick up and k 95 sts along right side of center panel to bound-off edge. Knit 1 row on WS.

Begin ridge pattern
Rows 1 and 3 (RS) K1, k2tog, k to end.
Row 2 K1, p to last 3 sts, p2tog, k1.
Ridge row 4 Knit.
Rep rows 1–4 until 2 sts rem. Bind off.

FINISHING
Weave in ends. Block to measurements.•

Swiss Shawl

Intermediate

MEASUREMENTS
Width along upper edge
77"/196.5cm
Length at center 31"/78.5cm

MATERIALS
Yarn
Any sport-weight mohair/silk blend, approx .88oz/25g balls, 229yd/209m per skein (2)
• 3 skeins in Lavender

Needles
• One size 7 (4.5mm) circular needle, 32"/80cm long, *or size to obtain gauge*

Notions
• Stitch markers

GAUGE
16 sts and 26 rows = 4"/10cm over eyelet pat (blocked) using size 7 (4.5mm) needles.
TAKE TIME TO CHECK YOUR GAUGE.

NOTES
1) Shawl is worked from the top down, starting with a garter tab.
2) First and last 3 sts are worked in garter st.
3) On WS, work (k1, p1) into each double yo.
4) Eyelet pattern may be worked from text or chart (see page 20).
5) When working increases into eyelet pat, if there are not enough sts to work ssk, yo twice, k2tog, then work these sts in St st.
6) Circular needle is used to accommodate large number of sts. Do *not* join.

EYELET PATTERN
(multiple of 8 sts plus 4)
Row 1 (RS) K4, *ssk, yo twice, k2tog, k4; rep from * to end.
Row 2 *P5, work (k1, p1) into double yo, p1; rep from * to last 4 sts, p4.
Rows 3 and 5 Knit.
Rows 4 and 6 Purl.
Row 7 Ssk, yo twice, k2tog, *k4, ssk, yo twice, k2tog; rep from * to end
Row 8 *P1, work (k1, p1) into double yo, p5; rep from * to last st, p1.
Rows 9 and 11 Knit.
Rows 10 and 12 Purl.
Rep rows 1–12 for eyelet pat.

SHAWL
Cast on 3 sts.
Knit 7 rows (on the last row, do *not* turn work). Rotate work clockwise.
Pick up and k 3 sts along left side edge into garter st ridges. Do *not* turn work. Rotate work clockwise.
Pick up and k 3 sts along cast-on edge—9 sts.

Set-Up Rows
Row 1 (RS) K3 (garter edge st), yo, k1, pm, k1 (center st), pm, k1, yo, k3 (garter edge st)—11 sts.
Row 2 K3, p2, sm, p1, sm, p2, k3.

Begin Increases
Row 1 (RS) K3, yo, k to marker, yo, sm, k1, sm, yo, k to marker, yo, k3—4 sts inc'd.
Row 2 K3, p to last 3 sts, k3.
Row 3 Rep row 1.
Row 4 Rep row 2.
Rows 5–10 Rep rows 1–4 once, then rows 1 and 2 once more—31 sts.

Begin Eyelet Pattern
Row 11 K3, yo, *work eyelet pat over next 12 sts as foll: k4, ssk, yo twice, k2tog, k4*, yo, sm, k1, sm, yo, rep between *'s once, yo, k3—35 sts.
Row 12 K3, p6, (k1, p1) into double yo, p6, sm, p1, sm, p6, (k1, p1) into double yo, p6, k3.
Rows 13–16 Rep rows 1–4 once—43 sts.
Row 17 K3, yo, *k3, ssk, yo twice, k2tog, k4, ssk, yo twice, k2tog, k3*, yo, sm, k1, sm, yo, rep between *'s once, yo, k3—47 sts.
Row 18 K3, *p5, (k1, p1) into double yo, p6, (k1, p1) into double yo, p5*, sm, p1, sm, rep between *'s once, k3.
Rows 19–22 Rep rows 1–4 once—55 sts.
Row 23 K3, yo, *k2, [ssk, yo twice, k2tog, k4] twice, ssk, yo twice, k2tog, k2*, yo, sm, k1, sm, yo, rep between *'s once, yo, k3—59 sts.
Row 24 K3, *p4, [(k1, p1) into double yo, p6] twice, (k1, p1) into double yo, p4*, sm, p1, sm, rep between *'s once, k3.
Cont in this way to inc 4 sts every RS row, working yo each side inside of k3 garter edge sts and before and after the center knit st, and working inc'd sts into eyelet pat when possible, until there are 343 sts, end with a WS row.

Edging
Row 1 (RS) K3, yo, k to marker, yo, sm, k1, sm, yo, k to last 3 sts, yo, k3—347 sts.
Row 2 Knit.
Work Picot bind off as foll: *Using knitted cast-on method, cast on 2 sts, bind off 4 sts, sl rem st back to LH needle; rep from * until all sts are bound-off.

Swiss Shawl

FINISHING
Weave in ends. Wet block to measurements, keeping integrity of natural wavy bound-off edge.•

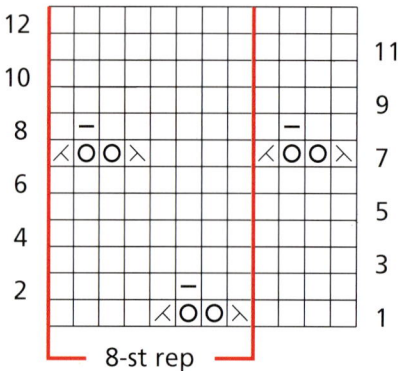

8-st rep

STITCH KEY

☐ k on RS, p on WS

⊟ p on RS, k on WS

◹ k2tog

◺ ssk

◯ yo

Garter Spine Shawl

Easy

MEASUREMENTS
Width along outer edge 68"/172.5cm
Length at center 32"/81cm

MATERIALS
Yarn
Any worsted-weight wool, approx 3½oz/100g skeins, 218yd/199m per skein 〔4〕
• 5 skeins in Variegated Green

Needles
• One size 7 (4.5mm) circular needle, 32"/80cm long, *or size to obtain gauge*

Notions
• Stitch markers

GAUGE
17 sts and 34 rows to 4"/10cm over garter st using size 7 (4.5mm) needles.
TAKE TIME TO CHECK YOUR GAUGE.

NOTE
A circular needle is used to accommodate large number of sts. Do *not* join.

SHAWL
Cast on 4 sts. Knit 1 row.
Row 1 K1, yo, k2, yo, k1—6 sts.
Row 2 Knit.
Row 3 K1, M1, k1, yo, k2, yo, k1, M1, k1—10 sts.
Row 4 Knit.
Row 5 K1, M1, k3, yo, pm, k2, pm, yo, k3, M1, k1—14 sts.
Row 6 Knit.
Row 7 K1, M1, k to marker, yo, sm, k2, sm, yo, k to last st, M1, k1—4 sts inc'd.
Rep last 2 rows 91 times more—382 sts.
Bind off loosely.

FINISHING
Weave in ends.
Block to measurements. •

Arrow Shawl

Intermediate

MEASUREMENTS
Width along upper edge
44"/111.5cm
Length at center 32"/81cm

MATERIALS
Yarn
Any DK-weight superwash wool, approx 3½oz/100g, 220yd/200m per skein
- 2 skeins in Light Green (A)
- 2 skeins in Dark Green (B)

Needle
- One size 7 (4.5mm) circular needle, 40"/100cm long, *or size to obtain gauge*

Notions
- Removable stitch marker

GAUGE
20 sts and 27 rows to 4"/10cm over k1, p1 rib using size 7 (4.5mm) needles.
TAKE TIME TO CHECK YOUR GAUGE.

NOTES
1) Slip the first st and knit the last st of every row.
2) Note that center marked st will always be the center st of the 5 or 9 sts worked in the decreases. Use a removable marker that can be moved up each RS row.
3) Circular needle is used to accommodate large number of sts. Do *not* join.

SHAWL
With A, cast on 351 sts. Place a marker on the center (176th) st.
Row 1 (WS) Sl 1, *p1, k1; rep from * to end.
Row 2 Sl 1, *k1, p1; rep from * to last 2 sts, k2.
Rep row 1 once more.

Begin Decrease Pattern 1
Dec row 1 (RS) Sl 1, *k1, p1; rep from * to 2 sts before center marked st, sl 3 tog, k2tog, pass slipped sts over, move marker up to st resulting from decrease, *p1, k1; rep from * to last st, k1—4 sts dec'd.
Row 2 Sl 1, *p1, k1; rep from * to end.

Rep rows 1 and 2 for 59 more times, AT THE SAME TIME, work stripe pat as foll:
4 rows A.
28 rows B.
12 rows A.
16 rows B.
22 rows A.
10 rows B.
26 rows A.
When stripe sequence and decrease pattern 1 are complete—111 sts.

Begin Decrease Pattern 2
Note Work 4 rows B, then work 22 rows A.
Dec row 1 (RS) Sl 1, *k1, p1; rep from * to 4 sts before center marked st, sl 5 tog, k4tog, pass slipped sts over, place marker on st resulting from decrease, *p1, k1; rep from * to last st, k1—8 sts dec'd.
Row 2 Sl 1, *p1, k1; rep from * to end.
Rep rows 1 and 2 twelve times more—7 sts. Cut yarn leaving a long tail. Thread tail through rem sts, draw up and secure.

FINISHING
Weave in ends. Block to measurements.•

Texture Trio Shawl

Intermediate

MEASUREMENTS
Width along upper edge 21"/53cm
Length at center 37"/94cm

MATERIALS
Yarn
Any DK-weight wool, approx 1¾oz/50g, 114yd/104m per skein
• 5 skeins in Red

Needles
• One pair size 6 (4mm) needles, *or size to obtain gauge*

Notions
• Stitch marker

GAUGE
22 sts and 32 rows to 4"/10cm over St st using size 6 (4mm) needles.
TAKE TIME TO CHECK YOUR GAUGE.

NOTE
As the staggered eyelet pattern is worked and sts are decreased each RS row, it is necessary to adjust the pattern to assure the eyelets are staggered.

STAGGERED EYELET PATTERN
(over a multiple of 4 sts plus 2)
Row 1 (RS) Knit.
Row 2 Purl.
Row 3 *K2, k2tog, yo; rep from * to last 2 sts, k2.
Row 4 Purl.
Rep rows 1–4 for staggered eyelet pat.

DOUBLE SEED
(over an even number of sts)
Row 1 (RS) *K1, p1; rep from * to end.
Row 2 *P1, k1; rep from * to end.
Row 3 *P1, k1; rep from * to end.
Row 4 *K1, p1; rep from * to end.
Rep rows 1–4 for double seed st.

SHAWL
Cast on 204 sts. Work in garter st (k every row) for 8 rows, dec 2 sts on last row—202 sts.
Next row (RS) K1, ssk, work in staggered eyelet pat to last 3 sts, k2tog, k1—2 sts dec'd.
Next row Work even in pat.
Rep last 2 rows until 4-row staggered eyelet pat has been worked 34 times, then work rows 1 and 2 once more—64 sts.
Next row (RS) K1, ssk, work double seed to last 3 sts, k2tog, k1—2 sts dec'd.
Next row (WS) P2, work double seed to last 2 sts, p2.
Rep last 2 rows 10 times more, then rep RS row once more—40 sts.

Next row (WS) P2, work 18 sts in pat, pm, work 18 sts in pat, p2.
Next row K1, ssk, k to 3 sts before marker, k2tog, k1, sm, k1, ssk, k to last 3 sts, k2tog, k1—4 sts dec'd.
Next row (WS) Knit.
Rep last 2 rows 7 times more—8 sts.
Next row (RS) K1, ssk, k2, k2tog, k1—6 sts.
Next row Knit.
Bind off as foll: K1, ssk, pass first st over 2nd to bind off, k2tog, bind off, k1, bind off. Fasten off last st.

FINISHING
Weave in ends. Block to measurements. •

Four-Triangle Shawl

Intermediate

MEASUREMENTS
Width around cast-on edge
80"/203cm
Length at center 18"/45.5cm

MATERIALS
Yarn
Any sport-weight superwash wool, approx 3½oz/100g, 360yd/330m per skein
• 2 skeins in Yellow

Needles
• One size 7 (4.5mm) circular needle, 32"/80cm long, *or size to obtain gauge*

Notions
• Stitch markers

GAUGE
20 sts and 28 rows to 4"/10cm over St st using size 7 (4.5mm) needle.
TAKE TIME TO CHECK YOUR GAUGE.

NOTES
1) Shawl is worked from the outer edge, with decreases creating 4 sections.
2) Circular needle is used to accommodate large number of sts. Do *not* join.

SHAWL
Using cable cast-on, cast on 410 sts.
Beg with a RS row, work 7 rows in rev St st (p on RS, k on WS).
Set-up row (WS) K5, pm, [k100, pm] 4 times, k5.

Begin Shaping and Ridge Pattern
Dec row 1 (RS) K5, sm, k2tog, [k to 2 sts before next marker, ssk, sm, k2tog] 3 times, k to 2 sts before marker, ssk, sm, k5—8 sts dec'd.
Rows 2 and 4 K5, sm, p to last 5 sts, k5.
Rows 3 and 5 Rep row 1.
Ridge row 6 Knit.
Rep rows 1–6 fifteen times more—26 sts.
Knit 2 rows.
Next dec row *K2tog; rep from * to end—13 sts.
Knit 1 row.
Next dec row [K2tog] 3 times, k1, [k2tog] 3 times—7 sts.
Knit 1 row.
Next dec row K2tog, k3, k2tog—5 sts.
Next dec row K2tog, k1, k2tog—3 sts.
Next row SK2P. Fasten off last st.

FINISHING
Weave in ends.
Block to measurements.•

Sideways Ridge Shawl

Easy

MEASUREMENTS
Width along upper edge 44"/111.5cm
Depth of triangle (unstretched) 17"/43cm
Depth of triangle (slightly stretched) 21"/53cm

MATERIALS
Yarn
Any DK-weight superwash wool, approx 1¾oz/50g, 130yd/118m per skein (3)
• 5 skeins in Light Green

Needles
• One pair size 5 (3.75mm) needles, *or size to obtain gauge*

Notions
• Removable stitch marker

GAUGE
32 sts and 31 rows to 4"/10cm over k2, p2 rib, slightly stretched, using size 5 (3.75mm) needles.
TAKE TIME TO CHECK YOUR GAUGE.

STITCH GLOSSARY
M1 open-knit Using LH needle, lift the yo strand inserting needle from the front to the back and k1 tbl into this strand to M1 open-knit.

M1 open-purl Using LH needle, lift the yo strand inserting needle from the front to the back and p1 tbl in this strand to M1 open-purl.

NOTE
This design is started at one elongated triangle point and sts are increased on one edge to the center of the triangle then decreased to the opposite elongated triangle point. If a larger shawl is desired, simply add increase rows until one half the length of desired piece across the top edge is achieved. Then decrease sts for the other side of the triangle.

SHAWL
Beg at the first elongated triangle point, cast on 4 sts.
Set-up row 1 (RS) K4.

Set-up row 2 P2, yo, p2.
Set-up row 3 K2, into yo work (p1 tbl, then M1 open-purl), k2.
Set-up row 4 P2, yo, k2, p2.
Set-up row 5 K2, p2, into yo work (k1 tbl, then M1 open-knit), k2.
Set-up row 6 P2, yo, p2, k2, p2—9 sts.

Begin Increases
Row 1 (RS) K2, *p2, k2; rep from * to the last 3 sts, into yo work (p1 tbl, then M1 open-purl), k2.
Row 2 P2, yo, *k2, p2; rep from * to end.
Row 3 K2, *p2, k2; rep from * to last 5 sts, p2, into yo work (k1 tbl, then M1 open-knit), k2.
Row 4 P2, yo, *p2, k2; rep from * to last 2 sts, p2—13 sts.
This increase method has one st increased at one edge every row.
Rep rows 1–4 thirty-nine times more, then row 1 once more—170 sts.
Place a removable st marker at beg of last RS row worked to mark one half of triangle top edge.

Begin Decreases
Set-up row 1 (WS) P2, SKP, *p2, k2; rep from * to last 2 sts, p2.
Dec row 2 *K2, p2; rep from * to last 5 sts, k2tog, yo, k2tog, k1—1 st dec'd.
Dec row 3 P2, k1, p2tog, work in established rib to end—1 st dec'd.
Rep dec rows 2 and 3 until 6 sts rem, end with a RS row.
Next row (WS) P2, k1, p2tog, p1—5 sts.
Last row K2, k2tog, k1—4 sts.
Bind off 1 st, p2tog then pull the first st on RH needle over the last st and fasten off.

FINISHING
Weave in ends. Lightly steam bock on WS, taking care not to stretch or press piece.•

Horizontal Stripes Shawl

Easy

MEASUREMENTS
Width along upper edge 42"/106.5cm
Length at center 24"/61cm

MATERIALS
Yarn
Any DK-weight superwash wool, approx 3½oz/100g, 306yd/280m per skein
- 2 skeins in Yellow (A)
- 1 skein in Red (B)

Needle
- One size 6 (4mm) circular needle, 40"/100cm long, *or size to obtain gauge*

Notions
- Stitch markers

GAUGE
19 sts and 32 rows to 4"/10cm over St st using size 6 (4mm) needle.
TAKE TIME TO CHECK YOUR GAUGE.

NOTE
Circular needle is used to accommodate large number of sts. Do *not* join.

SHAWL
With A, cast on 3 sts.
Rows 1 and 2 Knit.
Row 3 (RS) K1, M1, k1, M1, k1—5 sts.
Row 4 Knit.
Row 5 K1, M1, k to last st, M1, k1—2 sts inc'd.
Row 6 Knit.
Rep last 2 rows 5 times more—17 sts.

Begin Stripe Pattern
Note Knit 1 st into double yarn overs on WS rows, dropping extra wrap. Pattern inc's 2 sts every RS row inside markers.
Pat row 1 (RS) K8, pm, yo twice, k1, yo twice, pm, k8—19 sts.
Pat row 2 K8, sm, k1, p to 1 st before marker, k1, sm, k8.
Pat row 3 K8, sm, yo twice, k to marker, yo twice, sm, k8—2 sts inc'd.
Pat row 4 K8, sm, k1, p to 1 st before marker, k1, sm, k8.
Rep pat rows 3 and 4 eight times more—37 sts.
Note Join a 2nd ball of A to work garter st border on left edge.
Stripe row 1 With A, k8, sm, yo twice; with B, k to next marker; with 2nd ball of A, yo twice, sm, k8—2 sts inc'd.
Stripe row 2 With A, k8, sm, k1; with B, p to 1 st before marker; with A, k1, sm, k8.
Rep last 2 rows 3 times more—45 sts.
[With A, work pat rows 3 and 4 twelve times; work stripe rows 1 and 2 four times] 4 times, then with A, work pat rows 3 and 4 twelve times more—197 sts.
With A, knit 4 rows. Bind off.

FINISHING
Weave in ends. Block lightly to measurements.•

Color Swap Shawl

●●●●
Advanced

MEASUREMENTS
Width 70"/177.5cm
Length at center 20"/51cm

MATERIALS
Yarn
Any sock-weight wool, approx
1¾oz/50g, 170yd/155m per skein
• 1 skein in Lavender (A)
• 2 skeins in Purple (B)
• 3 skeins in Deep Purple (C)

Needles
• Two size 3 (3.25mm) circular needles, each 24"/60cm and 40"/100cm long, *or size to obtain gauge*
• One size 4 (3.5mm) circular needle, 40"/100cm long

Notions
• Stitch markers

GAUGE
24 sts and 42 rows to 4"/10cm over ridge pat using smaller needle.
TAKE TIME TO CHECK YOUR GAUGE.

RIDGE PATTERN
(over any number of sts)
Beg with a RS row, knit 1 row, purl 1 row, knit 2 rows.
Rep last 4 rows for ridge pat.

CHECK SLIP STITCH PATTERN
(over a multiple of 4 sts)
Note See pattern for assignment of MC and CC in each section.
Row 1 (RS) With CC, *sl 1, k3; rep from * to end.
Row 2 With CC, *p3, sl 1; rep from * to end.
Row 3 With MC, *k1, sl 1; rep from * to end.
Row 4 With MC, *sl 1, k1, sl 1, p1; rep from * to end.
Rows 5 and 6 Rep rows 1 and 2.
Row 7 With MC, knit.
Row 8 With MC, purl.
Rep rows 1–8 for check slip stitch pat.

NOTES
1) MC and CC change in each section of check slip stitch pattern.
2) Check slip stitch pattern is written out in section 1, in subsequent sections pattern can be worked from chart or text.
3) If working from chart, note that each row of chart represents 2 rows of knitting, both worked with color indicated at right edge of chart. Work the sts shown in working color and slip sts in opposite color. Note the stitch in the center of the box motif is worked as a knit on row 3, and also worked as a knit on the return row 4.
5) Sl sts wyib on RS rows and wyif on WS rows.
6) See pattern note regarding lining up subsequent repeats of check slip stitch pattern.

SHAWL
With shorter size 3 (3.25mm) needle and A, cast on 3 sts.
Row 1 (RS) K1, kfb, k1—4 sts.
Row 2 Purl.
Row 3 K1, kfb, k to end—5 sts.
Row 4 K3, kfb, k1—6 sts.

Ridge Pattern with Shaping
Row 1 (RS) K1, kfb, k to last 3 sts, ssk, k1.
Row 2 P to last 2 sts, purl into back then front of same st (pbf), p1—1 st inc'd.
Row 3 K1, kfb, k to end—1 st inc'd.
Row 4 K to last 2 sts, kfb, k1—1 st inc'd.
Rows 5–8 Rep rows 1–4.
Row 9 K1, kfb, k to last 3 sts, ssk, k1.
Row 10 P to last 2 sts, pbf—1 st inc'd.
Row 11 K1, kfb, k to last 3 sts, ssk, k1.
Row 12 K to last 2 sts, kfb, k1—1 st inc'd.
Rep rows 1–12 for ridge pat with shaping 6 times more, inc'ing 8 sts every 12 rows—62 sts.
Rep rows 1–12 once more, working [2 rows B, 2 rows A] 3 times—70 sts.
With B, rep rows 1–12 four times—102 sts.
With A, rep rows 9 and 10; with B, rep rows 11 and 12—104 sts.
Change to larger needle.
Next row (RS) With A, k1, kfb, k to end—105 sts.
Next row P to last 2 sts, pbf, p1—106 sts.

32

Color Swap Shawl

Check Slip Stitch Pattern

Shaping section 1

Note On subsequent repeats of check slip stitch pattern, final repeats may be incomplete. Work inc's and dec's into pat as indicated.

Using A as MC and C as CC, work as foll:

Row 1 With CC, k1, kfb, k4, *sl 1, k3; rep from * to last 4 sts, sl 1, ssk, k1.
Row 2 P2, *sl 1, p3; rep from * to last 8 sts, sl 1, p5, pbf, p1—1 st inc'd.
Row 3 With MC, k1, kfb, k7, *sl 1, k1; rep from * to last st, k1—1 st inc'd.
Row 4 P3, *sl 1, k1, sl 1, p1; rep from * to last 10 sts, sl 1, k7, kfb, k1—1 st inc'd.
Row 5 With CC, k1, kfb, k8, *sl 1, k3; rep from * to last 3 sts, sl 1, ssk.
Row 6 P1, *sl 1, p3; rep from * to last 12 sts, sl 1, p9, pbf, p1—1 st inc'd.
Row 7 With MC, k1, kfb, k to last 3 sts, k2tog, k1.
Row 8 K to last 2 sts, kfb, k1—1 st inc'd.
Row 9 With CC, k1, kfb, k4, *sl 1, k3; rep from * to last st, k1—1 st inc'd.
Row 10 P1, *p3, sl 1; rep from * to last 7 sts, p5, pbf, p1—1 st inc'd.
Row 11 With MC, k1, kfb, k7, *sl 1, k1; rep from * to last 4 sts, sl 1, ssk, k1.
Row 12 K2, sl 1, p1, *sl 1, k1, sl 1, p1; rep from * to last 9 sts, k7, kfb, k1—1 st inc'd.
Row 13 With CC, k1, kfb, k8, *sl 1, k3; rep from * to end—1 st inc'd.
Row 14 *P3, sl 1; rep from * to last 11 sts, p9, pbf, p1—1 st inc'd.
Row 15 With MC, k1, kfb, k to last 3 sts, ssk, k1.
Row 16 K to last 2 sts, kfb, k1—1 st inc'd.
Rep rows 1–16 for check slip stitch pat with shaping 2 times more, inc'ing 11 sts every 16 rows, then rep rows 1–8 once more—144 sts.

Shaping section 2

Note On all subsequent repeats of check slip stitch pattern, line up pattern rep with previous rows, working 2 additional 4-st repeats at beg of row every 8 rows as increasing allows and adjusting sts before first repeat as necessary. Final repeats may be incomplete. Work inc's and dec's into pat.

Next row (RS) With C, k1, kfb, k to end—145 sts.
Next row P to last 2 sts, pbf, p1—146 sts.
Using C as MC and A as CC, rep rows 1–16 as before 3 times, then rep rows 1–8 once more, working shaping into pat as before and inc'ing 11 sts every 16 rows—184 sts.

Shaping section 3

Next row (RS) With B, k1, kfb, k to end—185 sts.
Next row P to last 2 sts, pbf, p1—186 sts.
Using B as MC and C as CC, rep rows 1–16 as before 3 times, then rep rows 1–8 once more, working shaping into pat as before and inc'ing 11 sts every 16 rows—224 sts.

Shaping section 4

Next row (RS) With C, k1, kfb, k to end—225 sts.
Next row P to last 2 sts, pbf, p1—226 sts.
Using C as MC and B as CC, rep rows 1–16 as before 3 times, then rep rows 1–8 once more, working shaping into pat as before and inc'ing 11 sts every 16 rows—264 sts.

Final section

Change to longer size 3 (3.25mm) needle. Work with C to end as foll:
Row 1 (RS) K1, kfb, k to last 3 sts, ssk, k1.
Row 2 P to last 2 sts, pbf—265 sts.
Row 3 K 1, kfb, k to end—266 sts.
Row 4 K to last 2 sts, kfb, k1—267 sts.
Row 5 Rep row 1.
Row 6 Rep row 4—268 sts.
Rows 7 and 8 Rep rows 3 and 4—270 sts.
Row 9 Rep row 1.
Row 10 Rep row 4—271 sts.
Rows 11 and 12 Rep rows 9 and 10—272 sts.
Rows 13 and 14 Rep rows 3 and 4—274 sts.
Bind off loosely.

FINISHING

Weave in ends.
Block lightly to measurements.•

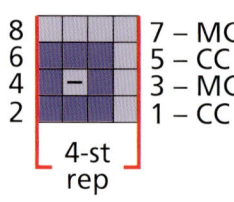

4-st rep

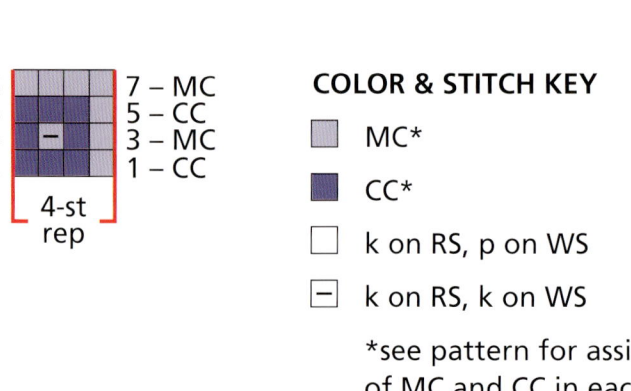

COLOR & STITCH KEY

☐ MC*

■ CC*

☐ k on RS, p on WS

⊟ k on RS, k on WS

*see pattern for assignment of MC and CC in each section

Open Waves Shawl

Easy

MEASUREMENTS
Width 75"/190cm
Depth 13"/33cm

MATERIALS
Yarn
Any DK-weight wool, approx 2.64oz/75g, 217yd/200m per skein
• 2 skeins in a Gray/Green/Brown Gradient

Needles
• One size 9 (5.5mm) circular needle, 40"/100cm long, *or size to obtain gauge*

Notions
• Stitch markers

GAUGE
20 sts and 36 rows to 4"/10cm over garter st using size 9 (5.5mm) needle.
TAKE TIME TO CHECK YOUR GAUGE.

NOTE
Circular needle is used to accommodate large number of sts. Do *not* join.

SHAWL
Cast on 3 sts. Knit 8 rows, turn work 90 degrees and pick up and k 5 sts along side edge, turn work and pick up and k 3 sts along cast-on edge—11 sts.
Next row (WS) K3, pm, k5, pm, k3.
Row 1 (RS) K3, sm, (k1, yo, k1) into next st, k to 1 st before marker, (k1, yo, k1) into next st, sm, k3—4 sts inc'd.
Row 2 K3, sm, yo, k to marker, yo, sm, k3—2 sts inc'd.
Rep rows 1 and 2 forty-five times more, then rep row 1 once more—291 sts.

Begin Edge Pattern
Row 1 (WS) K3, sm, yo, k4, *(k1, [p1, k1] twice) into next st, p5tog; rep from * to last 8 sts, (k1, [p1, k1] twice) into next st, k4, yo, k3.
Row 2 K3, sm, (k1, yo, k1) into next st, p to 1 st before marker, (k1, yo, k1) into next st, sm, k3.
Row 3 K3, sm, yo, k7, *(k1, [p1, k1] twice) into next st, p5tog; rep from * to last 11 sts, (k1, [p1, k1] twice) into next st, k7, yo, k3.
Row 4 K3, sm, (k1, yo, k1) into next st, p to 1 st before marker, (k1, yo, k1) into next st, sm, k3.
Row 5 Knit each st wrapping yarn around needle 3 times.
Row 6 Purl dropping extra wraps off needle.
Row 7 K2, *p5tog, (k1, [p1, k1] twice) into next st; rep from * to last 7 sts, p5tog, k2.
Row 8 Purl.
Bind off loosely purlwise.

FINISHING
Weave in ends. Block to measurements.•

Duality Shawl

Advanced

MEASUREMENTS
Width along shaped edge
55"/139.5cm
Length at center 25"/63.5cm

MATERIALS
Yarn
Any worsted-weight cotton/acrylic blend, approx 5.3oz/150g, 518yd/473m per skein (4)
• 1 skein in Self-Striping Earth Tones

Needle
• One size 8 (5mm) circular needle, 32"/80cm long, *or size to obtain gauges*

Notions
• Stitch markers

GAUGES
• 15 sts and 26 rows to 4"/10cm over welt pat using size 8 (5mm) needle.
• 13 sts and 22 rows to 4"/10cm over lace pat, after blocking, using size 8 (5mm) needle.
TAKE TIME TO CHECK YOUR GAUGES.

WELT PATTERN
Work 5 rows in St st (k on RS, p on WS), then 3 rows rev St st (p on RS, k on WS). Rep these 8 rows for welt pat.

LACE PATTERN
(over a multiple of 3 sts)
Row 1 (RS) *K1, yo, k2tog; rep from * to end.
Row 2 Purl.
Row 3 *K2tog, yo, k1; rep from * to end.
Row 4 Purl.
Rep rows 1–4 for lace pat.

NOTES
1) Slip all sts purlwise with yarn in front.
2) Shaping is worked by decreasing 1 st at end of RS rows. For a smooth edge, the first knit st following the slipped edge st on WS rows is worked with the yarn in front, creating a yarn over that is dropped on the next row.
3) The lace pattern is worked before the marker, and the welt pattern after the marker. As the rows are worked, the patterns shift, working more sts in the lace pattern until the entire row is worked in lace.
4) When shaping into lace pat, always work a yarn over paired with a decrease and vice versa, otherwise work sts in St st.
5) Circular needle is used to accommodate large number of sts. Do *not* join.

SHAWL
Cast on 129 sts loosely.
Row 1 (RS) *P1, k1; rep from * to last 3 sts, k3.
Row 2 Sl 1, wyif k1 (making yarn over by wrapping yarn over RH needle), k1, *p1, k1; rep from * to end.
Row 3 Sl 1, *k1, p1; rep from * to last 5 sts, k2tog, k1, drop yo, k1.
Row 4 Sl 1, wyif k1, k1, *k1, p1; rep from * to last st, k1.

Begin Lace and Welt Patterns
Row 5 (RS) Sl 1, k2, work row 1 of lace pat over 3 sts, pm, k to last 5 sts, k2tog, k1, drop yo, k1.
Row 6 Sl 1, wyif k1, p to last 3 sts, k3.
Row 7 Work in pats to marker, sm, k to last 5 sts, k2tog, k1, drop yo, k1.
Row 8 Rep row 6.
Row 9 Rep row 7.
Row 10 Sl 1, wyif k1, k to 3 sts before marker, p to last 3 sts, k3.
Row 11 Work in pats to marker, remove marker, cont lace pat over next 3 sts, pm, p to last 5 sts, k2tog, k1, drop yo, k1.
Row 12 Sl 1, wyif k1, k to marker, sm, p to last 3 sts, k3.
Row 13 Work to marker, remove marker, cont lace pat over next 3 sts, pm, k to last 5 sts, k2tog, k1, drop yo, k1.
Rows 14–20 Rep rows 6–12.
Rep rows 13–20 ten times more, then rep rows 13–15 once more—78 sts. Marker will be 3 sts from end of row, remove marker.
Cont in lace pat only between the selvage sts each side
Row 104 (WS) Sl 1, wyif k1, k1, p to last 3 sts, k3.
Row 105 Sl 1, k2, work in lace pat to last 5 sts, k2tog, k1, drop yo, k1.
Rep last 2 rows until 4 sts rem, end with a RS row.
Next row (WS) Sl 1, k to end.
Next row Sl 1, k2tog, k1—3 sts.
Next row Sl 1, k to end.
Next row Sl 1, k2tog—2 sts.
Next row K2tog. Fasten off last st.

FINISHING
Weave in ends. Block to measurements.•

Garter & Lace Shawl

Intermediate

MEASUREMENTS
Width 54"/137cm
Length 14"/35.5cm

MATERIALS
Yarn
Any DK-weight wool, approx 1¾oz/50g, 136yd/124m per skein (3)
• 4 skeins in Purple

NEEDLES
• One each size 5 and 7 (3.75 and 4.5mm) circular needle, 32"/80cm long, *or size to obtain gauge*

Notions
• Stitch marker

GAUGE
16 sts and 40 rows to 4"/10cm over garter st using larger needles.
TAKE TIME TO CHECK YOUR GAUGE.

SHORT ROW WRAP & TURN (w&t)
1) Wyib, sl next st purlwise.
2) Move yarn between the needles to the front.
3) Sl the same st back to LH needle. Turn work. One st is wrapped.
4) When working the wrapped st, insert RH needle under the wrap and work it tog with the corresponding st on needle.
Note It is not necessary to pick up wraps in garter stitch, just knit wrapped sts as usual.

NOTE
Shawl is worked from lower edge and shaped with short rows.

SHAWL
With smaller needle, work picot edge cast-on as foll:
*[Cast on 5 sts using knitted cast-on, bind off 2 sts, sl 1 st back to LH needle] twice, cast on 10 sts using knitted cast-on, bind off 2 sts, sl 1 st back to LH needle (14 sts cast on); rep from * 14 times more—210 sts.
Cast on 5 sts using knitted cast-on, bind off 2 sts, sl 1 st back to LH needle, cast on 2 sts using knitted cast-on—215 sts.
Next 4 rows Sl 1, k to end.

Lace Section
Note Lace section may be worked from chart or written instructions.
Row 1 (WS) Sl 1, k1, *k1, p13; rep from * to last 3 sts, k3.
Row 2 Sl 1, k1, p1, *k3, k2tog, yo, k3, yo, ssk, k3, p1; rep from * to last 2 sts, k2.
Rows 3 and 5 Rep row 1.
Row 4 Sl 1, k1, p1, *k2, k2tog, yo, k5, yo, ssk, k2, p1; rep from * to last 2 sts, k2.
Row 6 Sl 1, k1, p1, *k1, k2tog, yo, k7, yo, ssk, k1, p1; rep from * to last 2 sts, k2.
Row 7 Sl 1, k1, *k1, p5, k3, p5; rep from * to last 3 sts, k3.
Row 8 Sl 1, k1, p1, *k2tog, yo, k3, p3, k3, yo, ssk, p1; rep from * to last 2 sts, k2.
Rep rows 1–8 for lace section twice more.

Garter Body
Change to larger needle.
Row 1 (WS) Sl 1, kfb, k to end—216 sts.
Row 2 Sl 1, k1,*yo, k2tog; rep from * to end.
Row 3 Sl 1, k107, pm, k108.

Begin short row shaping
Short row 1 (RS) Sl 1, k to marker, sm, k2, w&t.
Short row 2 (WS) K to marker, sm, k2, w&t.
Short row 3 K to 1 st beyond previously wrapped st, w&t.
Rep short row 3 until all sts have been worked each side of marker.
Bind off loosely.

FINISHING
Weave in ends. Block to measurements, pinning out points along cast-on edge.•

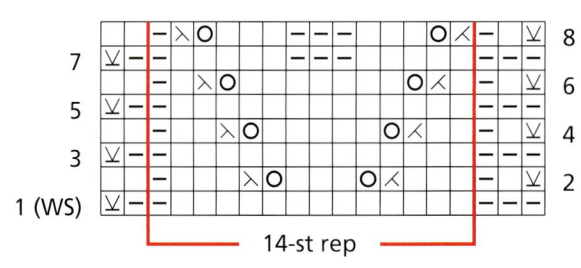

STITCH KEY
☐ k on RS, p on WS
⊟ p on RS, k on WS
⋋ k2tog
⋌ ssk
○ yo
⋁ slip 1 wyib on RS, slip 1 wyif on WS

Rainbow Shawl

Easy

MEASUREMENTS
Width along outer edge 66"/167.5cm
Length at center 26½"/67.5cm

MATERIALS
Any worsted-weight cotton/acrylic blend, approx 5.3oz/150g, 481yd/440m per skein (4)
• 1 skein in Self-Striping Rainbow Colors

Needles
• One size 8 (5mm) circular needle, 40"/100cm long, *or size to obtain gauge*

Notions
• Stitch marker

GAUGE
17 sts and 32 rows to 4"/10cm over garter st using size 8 (5mm) needle.
TAKE TIME TO CHECK YOUR GAUGE.

NOTES
1) Slip sts at end of rows purlwise wyif.
2) Circular needle is used to accommodate large number of sts. Do *not* join.

SHAWL
Cast on 8 sts.
Set-up row 1 K7, sl 1.
Set-up row 2 Rep row 1.

Begin Shaping
Row 1 (RS) K2, [yo, k1] twice, pm, [k1, yo] twice, k1, sl 1.
Row 2 K to last st, sl 1.
Row 3 K2, yo, k to 1 st before marker, yo, k1, sm, k1, yo, k to last 2 sts, yo, k1, sl 1—4 sts inc'd.
Rep rows 2 and 3 until piece measures 4"/10cm from beg, end with a RS row.

Eyelet sequence
Eyelet row 1 (WS) K3, p to 2 sts before marker, k2, sm, k2, p to last 3 sts, k2, sl 1.
Eyelet row 2 (RS) K2, yo, *k2tog, yo; rep from * to 2 sts before marker, yo, k2tog, sm, k1, yo, *k2tog, yo; rep from * to last 3 sts, yo, k2tog, sl 1—2 sts inc'd.
Eyelet row 3 K3, p to 2 sts before marker, k2, sm, k2, p to last 3 sts, k2, sl 1.
Working as before, [rep rows 2 and 3 for 2"/5cm, then work eyelet rows 1–3] twice, then rep rows 2 and 3 for 4"/10cm, work eyelet row 1–3 once more. [Rep rows 2 and 3 for 2"/5cm, then work eyelet rows 1–3] twice more.
Rep rows 2 and 3 for 2"/5cm more. Bind off loosely.

FINISHING
Weave in ends. Block to measurements.•